Reclaiming Your Identity In Christ

AMMIE BOUWMAN

Reclaiming Your Identity In Christ
Copyright © 2021 by Ammie Bouwman

All rights reserved.
Published in the United States by Ammie Bouwman
Unless otherwise noted, Scripture quotations are from the Holy Bible, New International Version. NIV Copyright. Used by Permission.
All rights reserved worldwide.
ISBN 9798454079093
Printed in the United States of America.

"So God created mankind in his own image,
in the image of God he created them;
male and female he created them."

Genesis 1:27

Contents

Introduction

Step 1 — When We Ask God Why? - Understanding His Original Design

Step 2 — How Did I Get Here? - Understanding Your Past

Step 3 — How Do I Move Forward? - Reclaiming Your Identity

Step 4 — How Do I Keep My Identity? - Understanding Dominion And Authority

Step 5 — How Do I Fight? - Putting On The Full Armor Of God

Step 6   Grace Over Guilt – You Can Always Return To The Path

Step 7   Seed, Time, And Harvest – Growing in God

Closing Thoughts

Acknowledgements

Class Notes

Introduction

Why is it always easier to believe the negative? I know for me, I use to shrink away at a compliment, shrug off the affirmation and send packing any praise. But the negative? I sealed that in and tucked it away for rainy days. Some days I would play it on repeat until I was swimming in a sea of regret; "Why did I do that? Why did I eat that? Why can't I have that moment back? Am I really loved? Who am I?"

And while I walked around each day, clean from head to toe with a shower and laundered clothes, I never felt clean on the inside. Guilt was my friend, and grace seemed more like a far-away concept than something I could ever hold in my hand, let alone my heart.

Somewhere along the line, my perception was altered. The brokenness of this world broke in and changed the way I viewed life and viewed myself. When I looked in the mirror, I didn't see this person created in God's image who was loved, cherished, and created for a purpose. I saw a mistake. I saw a lifetime of missed opportunities and failed chances that I would never get back.

Every mistake, every hurt, wrong turn, and blown stop sign were constant reminders that this was who I was, and there was no use trying to be somebody else. I might as well accept that this is my life and that if there is a God, He has forgotten about me.

Is this you today? Are you traveling a road of confusion? Are you playing on repeat every wrong choice you have ever made and living in the past? If you no longer recognize the person looking back at you in the mirror, then there's a reason you are holding onto this book. Somewhere along the line, you stopped believing that you are created in God's image. You stopped believing that you are forgiven. You stopped believing in the unlimited grace that is offered to us when we reach out our hands. Somewhere you stepped away from the plan and purpose God has for you, and you stopped believing His Truth.

But what I love about Jesus is that we can always return. When we get that revelation of truth and repent of our past mistakes, rebuke the enemy and his plans, renounce the devil's efforts to continue to work in our lives, and receive the forgiveness and transformational truth that only comes from Jesus Christ. We can get back on His path. We can once and for all stop believing the negative and step into the life He has had planned for us all along. We can look in the mirror and remember who we truly are, sons and daughters of the highest King. Are you ready? Let's do this together, one step at a time.

If you are able, I'd like you to look at this book as a seven-week journey. Give yourself some time. Don't rush through the steps. The number seven is a number of completeness and perfection, so look at these next seven weeks and seven steps as a way for God to start a perfect work in you that He will complete in you in His perfect timing and for His Glory.

Inside of each week is seven baby steps, so each day, you will be touching this book in some way and allowing God's Truth to penetrate your life. Each day there will be something to read, some truth to meditate on, and something to journal. Allow the Holy Spirit to work in your heart, answer your questions, and help you to move forward. It has taken time for you to get where you are today. Give yourself grace and time to roll your life back onto God's path and reclaim your identity in Christ. I'm praying for you. Let's begin.

Ammie Bouwman

Step 1

When We Ask God Why? - Understanding His Original Design

Abraham Lincoln once said, "In giving freedom to the slave, we assure freedom to the free -- honorable alike in what we give, and what we preserve. We shall nobly save, or meanly lose, the last best, hope of earth." This beautiful version of freedom, however, was not Pharaoh's philosophy in Eqypt in 1290 B.C. He ruled without disregard for the Israelites, who eventually exchanged their freedom for food during the seven-year famine that ravaged Egypt and the surrounding lands. But if you don't know the story, let me take you back to Exodus in the Bible and show you "one of the greatest miracles of God's care for his people in the Old Testament - the Israelites being freed from slavery and leaving Egypt." (Introduction of Exodus - NIV)

I think most people, regardless of their faith, have heard of Moses. He's the man who brought the Israelites out of Egypt and helped them cross the Red Sea on dry ground. But suppose you didn't hear about him in Sunday school or read about him in the Bible. In that case, you may have seen the movie "The Ten Commandments" with Charlton Heston and Yul Brenner that came out in 1956 or the newer version "Exodus: Gods and Kings" with Christian Bale and Joel Edgerton that was released in 2014.

What you may not have known, and where the story gets interesting, was that Moses was born during a time when by the law of Pharaoh, every Hebrew baby boy was born to be killed. Pharaoh and the Egyptians were worried about the growing number of Israelites and that they would eventually outnumber them and join their enemies to fight against them.

But God had such an extraordinary plan for Moses's life that he was spared. Baby Moses was taken to the Nile River by his sister, hoping that he wouldn't be found - which he was. "Then Pharaoh's daughter went down to the Nile to bathe, and her attendants were walking along the river bank. She saw the basket among the reeds and sent her slave girl to get it. She opened it and saw the baby. He was crying, and she felt sorry for him. 'This is one of the Hebrew babies,' she said." (Exodus 1:5-6 NIV)

Fast forward, and Moses, born a Hebrew slave, was raised in the palace of Pharaoh, treated like royalty and lived the life of a Prince. Eventually, the truth was revealed that He was Hebrew and, becoming curious, went out to his own people and watched them at their hard labor. After witnessing an Egyptian beating a Hebrew, Moses killed the Egyptian and hid his body in the sand. When he realized that he had been seen, Moses fled to Midian and started a new life.

I bet you're wondering, "Ok, what does this have to do with Abraham Lincoln, freedom, slavery, reclaiming my identity, and understanding God's original design?" Well, I have one word for you: perspective. Depending on how you look at something is how you will see the world. It's how you will look at your life and interpret the answers when you ask God why.

If you keep reading in Exodus, you'll see that God came to Moses, in a burning bush no less - and commissioned him to go back to Egypt to free His people. And Moses not only returned to where his life began, facing the people that he had called family, but was part of one of the greatest exodus stories ever recorded - releasing a people from bondage and starting them on a journey towards freedom.

But it was not easy leading two million Hebrews out of Egypt. It was not easy following a man you didn't know. It was not easy leaving behind the only home you have ever known - even if you were a slave. Sometimes it would've been easier to go back to building bricks.

Hence my point = perspective. From Pharoah's perspective, this God was taking his slave labor. How would he build the bricks to grow his kingdom? From the Israelites perspective, they were finally receiving their freedom but were frustrated following Moses in the desert. From Moses's perspective, He was trying to do what God commissioned him to do, but felt like a failure at every turn and was frustrated leading a group of people who kept complaining about the food, the journey, and the rules.

How many times do you think they all cried out, "Why?" How many times do you think they blamed God? This is where we stop for a moment and look at things from God's perspective. You see, God's original design was not for the Israelites to exchange their freedom for food. God's original plan was not for killing Hebrew baby boys and for an entire race of people to be enslaved by the government. God's original design was not for war but peace: shalom; nothing missing and nothing broken. Everything that was transpiring was not part of

God's plan at all.

So let's go back to the beginning. Before Exodus, there was Genesis. In the beginning, God created the heavens and the earth. He created day and night, separated water from the sky, and created dry ground and seas. He made vegetation on the land and stars and planets in the sky. He filled the water with living creatures and the sky with birds and blessed them. He created living creatures and wild animals and livestock, and then He created man and woman in His image, to rule over the fish of the sea and the birds of the air, over the livestock, over all the earth. When He finished His work by the seventh day, He rested. He blessed the day and made it holy.

This strategic planning and care were not from a God who would later introduce global warming, sex trafficking, and cancer. No! Our demise came with a whisper and the words, "Did God really say?" When Eve ate the apple, sin entered the world, and the enemy - Satan, took the dominion and authority that God gave us as His image-bearers. Everything changed, and God's original design - to be in fellowship with us, to be with us-was halted until Jesus arrived on the scene. Jesus was the key to restoring the relationship with God. Jesus was the key to canceling the works of Satan. Jesus was the key to eradicating sin and paying the ultimate penalty on our behalf so that we could have forgiveness of sin and everlasting life.

Even today, in 2021, God is still restoring us to Himself. The hour is growing closer when Jesus will return and take us home - to our eternal home. But so many of us are still asking God why? So many of us are still stuck in the perspective that God is the cause of the world's problems. So many are still forgetting to go back to the beginning and see His original design. That we were created in His image, given dominion and authority in this world, and that He sent His son to bridge the gap and restore us into fellowship with Him. What did Abraham Lincoln mean when he said, "In giving freedom to the slave, we assure freedom to the free -- honorable alike in what we give, and what we preserve. We shall nobly save, or meanly lose, the last best, hope of earth?" It means we have to change our perspective. Lincoln knew that he could not escape history or the horrendous acts that were carried out against the African American people. But he said, "we hold the power and bear the responsibility."

We, too, have the responsibility and hold the power, and it's time to believe it. In Jesus, we can reclaim who we are and Whose we are and know that God's Word promises us abundant life without a shadow of a doubt. Like the Israelites, we need to stop forgetting that we are no longer slaves and step into the promised land. We must stop asking God why and understand God's original design and what He has been doing since the garden to restore us to Himself. Instead of fighting against God, we need to fight the true enemy responsible for distracting us away from our identity in Christ. It's time to reclaim it. It's time to stop asking why and start believing we are free! It is the last, best hope of this earth.

Baby Step 1

Take a few moments and write out how you see yourself as of today. Be honest. We want to shine God's Light into the dark areas of our lives and into every negative thought and untruth.

_____
_____
_____
_____
_____
_____
_____
_____
_____
_____

How do you see yourself?

Baby Step 2

After reading about God's original design for this world, are there things in your life that you have been blaming Him for? Have you questioned Him in the past and asked Why? If so, write God a letter and tell Him what those things are. He's big enough to handle it. Share with Him what you're feeling.

Dear God,

Baby Step 3

Today, read Genesis Chapter 1, and answer the following questions:

1. How did God create the world? _____

2. In whose image did He create mankind? _____

3. What commission did He give to mankind? _____
   _____

4. What did God give us? _____

5. After God saw all that He had made, how did He describe it? _____
   _____

Meditate on these verses. Don't rush past the simplicity of the words used. In His exceedingly glorious and all-powerful way, He spoke the world into existence and created everything perfectly. Amen!

Baby Step 4

Today, read Genesis Chapter 2, and answer the following questions:

1. What did God do on the seventh day? _____

2. How was man formed? _____

3. How was woman formed? _____

4. What was woman called? _____

5. Was there shame in the garden? _____
_____

Meditate on these verses. Pay careful attention to the perfection God created. There was no shame, no division, no loneliness - nothing missing and nothing broken. It was God's perfect shalom - peace! This was God's original design. This was how He created the world. It was perfect.

Baby Step 5

Today, read Genesis Chapter 3, and answer the following questions:

1. What came on the scene in the first verse? _____

2. What did he say to the woman? _____ _____

3. What was the "lie?"_____

4. What was the first thing Adam and Eve did after eating the fruit?
_____
5. What were the consequences? _____
_____

Meditate on these verses. Can you see that the brokeness of today's world is the direct result of sin? After reading these chapters, do you better understand God's original design and His plan for us? Who was in charge of the first deception? Is he still deceiving the world today? Is he still saying to us:
"Did God really say?"

Baby Step 6

So my questions for you to meditate on today are these: If we're created in God's image, and have a creative spirit just like Him, then how are we similar? Are we able to speak things into existence? Are we saying over ourselves and those we love life-giving words, or are we questioning God's ability and His truth? Are we spending our time asking God why and blaming Him for the brokenness of this world? Are we listening to the enemy and all of his lies?

Meditate on this verse today:

"You who fear him, trust in the LORD - he is their help and shield." ~ PSALM 115:11

Baby Step 7

Over the last seven days, what truth has been revealed to you? Do you have a better understanding of God's original design? Use the journal space below to write out some new truths and what God has shown you.

Step 2

How Did I Get Here? - Understanding Your Past

Most of us don't drive around aimlessly. We often use landmarks, a GPS, or map out our journeys for the most direct route. We like to know where we're going and don't want to use our resources like gas and time unnecessarily. It's the same in real life. It's not our goal to walk around in a state of disorientation and confusion, second-guessing our path and questioning every single step we take.

But often, our life feels less like a car ride and more like we've been dropped into the ocean. We are tossed to and fro with each swell, clamoring for air and trying to regain our position. And when we think we can see land, another wave hits us, and we are washed off course. We try and swim and become weak, discouraged, and eventually, give up on our own strength.

We say to ourselves, "How did I get here?" and can't believe how far off course we are. We succumb to the new route and say, "well, I guess this was God's will," or we even question there is a God and blame Him for His blatant lack of interest in our lives.

If you were to take a moment and evaluate your current longitude and latitude, how far off course are you? Do you feel disconnected from God and that He has somehow been watching you float in a sea of depression, anxiety, and hopelessness and hasn't even cared?

Part of getting back on course is understanding where you are. I don't know how many times my husband and I have been out driving, took some wrong turns, and had to stop to get out the map. I won't tell you who encouraged him to do that, lol, but I will say that we had to figure out what town we were in, what road we were traveling, what direction we were going so we could get our bearings, change course, and get back home.

It's the same in our journey of life. Yes, maybe you've taken some wrong roads. Perhaps you've lost your way. Maybe some detours weren't even your fault. But it's time to stop the car, find out where you are, and get back on the road that leads to home - God!

In my journey, I had to go back, not only to where I stepped off the path but where my identity shifted. For me, that was my parent's divorce. Until that day, when they sat me down and told me that their marriage was ending, I was confident of the road that I was on. I knew God loved me and that I was His child. Now, I know everyone is different, and maybe your story doesn't hold even a few years of a constant, stable foundation. And that's why we started with understanding God's original design.

He planned that each person coming into this world would have two loving parents, equally yoked, standing on a solid foundation of peace, love, security, and a full awareness of God. They would teach their children about who they are, who God is, and the unique plan God has for them. But because of sin, we have broken beginnings, shattered families, abuse, neglect, and suitcase after suitcase of pain that we carry around. We let each swell take us, almost drowning us and spitting us out further and further away from God and

His original design.

Who's fault is that? Well, we could blame Adam and Eve. We could go back to the garden when Satan came and tempted them with the delicious fruit. But it doesn't make sense to spend our lives blaming others. We've already lost too much time blaming our parents, our friends, our spouses, that person that hurt you, robbed you of one too many days, and kept you trapped beneath the wreckage of your life.

We get to this point in our journey where we acknowledge that we've had pain, we've had disappointments, we've gone through things that should've never happened, and we have to make a decision. We can scream out loud, "Oh, I know how I've got here. They did this to me. He did this. She did this. My life could be so different. I could be so different." Or, we can say, "I wonder what happened to them to make them do this to me?"

You see, we are all broken. We are all one step away from dark pathways, human tragedy, suffering, loss, and death. But when we lift our eyes and look past the broken world, we can see someone is standing in the gap. He came to cancel the plans of the enemy. He came to restore God's original design. He came to redeem the lost and broken. He came to bridge the distance between God and man. And He did that with a cross.

We can keep allowing the enemy to send the storm. We can keep circling in the desert, wanting to return to our Egypt and live as slaves. We can keep looking down and not seeing who is standing in front of us with His hand held out, wanting us to know who we truly are. Or, we can choose forgiveness. We can choose love. We can choose to surrender our past hurts and regret and lay them all down at the foot of the cross. Whatever it is, it is our choice. It is your choice. What will you choose?

If we are going to reclaim our identity, it's time to set aside our old way of thinking. It's time to let go of whatever we're still hanging onto and let God work and move. We can try and understand why that person hurt us, their motives, how they could do that, and how they can live with themselves. And maybe they're not. Perhaps they are living in their own ocean of disappointment and regret and living underneath the swells. We can only hope they will change their lives and find their way back to God.

And, we can keep kicking ourselves for the mistakes we've made and every wrong turn. But trust me, there are some things we will never fully understand. Ultimately, we've come to a crossroads. We stand here today with a choice. We can go backward and keep reliving all the pain. We can move sideways and never experience the whole adventure. Or we can set our course for True North, living daily in the arms of Jesus and trusting in Him until He comes again to take us home.

You see, we understand our past and where we've come from, and how we've gotten here so we can change direction. So we can see what we want to do differently. Soren Kierkegaard once wrote, "Life can only be understood backwards, but it must be lived forwards." Are you ready to move forward? If so, it's time to turn the page.

Baby Step 1

Take a few moments and write out the names of the people who hurt you. Are you still holding onto unforgiveness? If your name is on that list, it's time to forgive yourself. Lay it all down at the foot of the cross.

_____

_____

_____

_____

_____

_____

_____

_____

_____

Baby Step 2

Look again at the list of names on your list. Write a few sentences to each one, extending forgiveness. Ask God to help you at this moment not only to forgive but let go.

Dear God,

Baby Step 3

Today, read Luke Chapter 23:26-43, and answer the following questions:

1. How many times was forgiveness talked about? _____

2. Who did Jesus forgive? _____

3. What do you think Jesus meant when He said, "Father forgive them?" ____
_____

4. What does it mean to you to receive Jesus' forgiveness? _____
_____

5. After reading this passage, is there anyone you are still holding back from forgiving? _____

Meditate on these verses. When we hold back forgiveness, we are nullifying the work Jesus did on the cross. We are saying what He went through was not enough. Today, receive His sweet forgiveness, and offer up the same forgiveness He offers you.

Baby Step 4

Today, read Matthew 18:21-35 and answer the following questions:

1. What was the Parable about? _____

2. What was Jesus really saying in this story? _____
_____

3. What does the 70 x 7 represent?_____

4. Do you feel like you cannot offer forgiveness even one more time? Does this parable change things for you? _____

5. What does unforgiveness cost you? What does forgiveness cost you?____
_____

Meditate on these verses. As we read about forgiving the people in our past, we can learn how to forgive those who have not yet hurt us. There is true freedom in living in love, forgiving others the way Jesus forgive us, and letting go of human hurt.

Baby Step 5

Today, are you still struggling with how God can love you despite your past brokenness and sin? Do you still feel lost, damaged, and misunderstood? Read Mark 5:1-20, then read the excerpt below and answer the questions.

Why did Jesus cross the lake in the first place? He traveled to help one man. A man who was possessed and so out of control that those around him tried to chain him. But even chains couldn't hold him. When I think of this story, I put myself in this man's sandals. I was so lost, so out of my mind, that I didn't make good decisions, and so hopeless that I wanted to take my own life. And even while Jesus was on His way, the enemy was trying to block Him from coming. He caused a storm, and the boat rocked, and the wind blew. But God! Jesus knew what was happening and rebuked the wind and calmed the seas. He crossed the lake anyway. And He didn't come to save thousands; He came to save just me, and He's come to save you.

1. Do you believe that Jesus is actively pursuing you ? _____

2. Do you believe He would cross the lake just for you? Why or why not.
   _____
   _____

3. What is Jesus rescuing you from?_____

4. Read Mark 4:35-41 for the full story of the storm.

5. Do you believe that Jesus can calm the storms in your life caused by the enemy?
   _____

Baby Step 6

So my questions for you to meditate on today are: What is your current longitude and latitude? Do you still feel like you are off-course? Do you feel ready to move forward into everything that God has planned for you? Are you prepared to leave your past behind?

Meditate on this verse today:

"Not that I have already attained, or am already perfected; but I press
on, that I may lay hold of that for which Christ Jesus has also laid hold of me. I do not count myself to have apprehended; but one thing I do, forgetting those things which are behind and reaching forward to those things which are ahead, I press toward the goal for the prize of the upward call of God in Christ Jesus."
~ Philippians 3:12-14 (NKJV)

Baby Step 7

Over the last seven days, what truth has been revealed to you? Do you have a better understanding of your past and how you need to let it go? Use the journal space below to write out some new truths and what God has shown you.

Step 3

How Do I Move Forward? - Reclaiming Your Identity

This is always the most challenging part. It's like we're sitting on the edge of the bed, knowing we have to get up and start moving but are overwhelmed with the thoughts, "What should I do first?" We can't see the bottom of the list and know we don't have the energy it's going to take and sometimes just want to get back into bed and say, "Maybe tomorrow. Maybe tomorrow will be the day." Well, this is why you're reading this. This is why we're taking one step at a time, holding each other accountable, making this journey together. Sometimes you need that person to encourage you and say, "It's okay, let's tackle it together. Let's chip away at that list."

So let's take a minute and recap. We've looked at God's original design and have a better understanding of why we struggle in this world. We know now that it's broken, filled with broken people, and that we're all affected by sin. This ebb and blow of brokenness can dictate our steps if we don't look to God's truth and understand how he's been working at restoring us to Himself. This overall truth needs to stay with us as we move forward. This needs to be the base of our foundation as we rebuild and reclaim our identity.

Up until today, we may have let the world define who we are. And we as people like to label things and fit them neatly into the compartments of our minds. We think by labeling something, we have a better understanding of it, so we get out those label makers and define our world. I believe this starts at a young age, and we're raised labeling and defining. Have you ever looked at someone who has mismatched clothes on or wearing bright colors in their hair? We may look at them differently because they do not fit into any of our mental boxes. And because they are different from us, we label or "judge" when they are just expressing their individuality and uniqueness.

Here's the thing, positive labels are lovely and reinforce our identity and who we think we are. There is confidence in the positive characteristics, and the cycle is an enjoyable, forward motion. It feels okay when we label ourselves:

- successful
- organized
- nurturing
- good-hearted
- super mom

But the negative labels are equally reinforced. There is the "lack" that we feel. Lack of confidence. Lack of purpose. Lack of forward motion when we carry the labels:
- ugly
- undesirable
- incompetent
- slow learner

- broken
- addict
- divorced

Often the labels we struggle with the most are the ones we've gotten from other people. Something is said to us in passing, a wrong diagnosis, a harsh word, a judgment or observation, and it sticks and never goes away. Let me tell you a little secret. The devil loves labels. And he uses these labels to keep up from stepping onto the realization of who we are in Jesus Christ. What we forget is that these labels are coming from broken people, broken people just like us. Yet we take their lies and labels and sew it to ourselves and wear it like a badge. Before we know it, we're covered with these sticky-note labels, filled with words of the world, believing that this is who we are.

Here's where it's time to get off the edge of the bed. Here's where we take another step forward and tackle that list that you've had covering your heart. It's time to take off the sticky notes, one by one. Let them all go. You are NOT what the world says you are. You are not who the devil says you are. You don't have to stay where you are anymore. It's time to step into everything that God has in store for you and receive His identity. The one He has had for you all along.

Neil T. Anderson wrote an influential book called *Who I Am In Christ*. He tells us that "the most important belief about ourselves is that we are children of God and that being His child is a right given to us by God Himself." He goes on to give us this imagery of our beginnings and that we are we are all related, or 'in Adam.' Between descendants, there exists a blood relationship, born of the flesh and the will of mankind. "But we have to remember that even though sin entered the world, God has been restoring us back to Himself since Adam. We don't have to live "in the world," believing what man says and clinging to the brokenness. We can hang onto God's promises, and who He says we are, in Jesus Christ: "Yet to all who received him, to those who believed in his name, he gave the right to become children of God - children born not of natural descent, nor of human decision or a husband's will, but born of God." ~ John 1:12,13

These words tell us that no matter your beginning, your past, and how you got to today, you can choose to believe and remember that you are a child of God. You can choose to believe what God's Word says about you and no longer wear the sticky notes of this world. You can choose to believe that you were bought at a price and loved so much that God sacrificed His only Son on a cross. Just for you. So you can live in this freedom and have life everlasting. So you can live securely in your identity and know who you are—the son or daughter of the Highest King.

Did you recognize the repeated word? Choose. We have to make a choice. I can show you the door. I can encourage you to walk through it. I call tell you there is so much freedom when you walk through. But you have to take the steps. You have to grab the handle. You have to turn the knob and open the door. He gives each of us a choice.

And that's one of the things I love most about Him. Nothing is forced. He doesn't strong-arm me. He simply invites me with this unconditional love, patience and understanding that I have never experienced anywhere else in my life. I feel His acceptance despite my sin and imperfection. He loves me right where I am and invites me into His truth to learn how to live in a broken world with broken people and love them as He loves me.

So how do we walk this out? How do we apply these truths to our lives and reclaim our identity? One step at a time. As we learn to love ourselves and remember who we are, we can better love our family, friends, those in our community, and the people in our past who have hurt us. Jesus tells us this in John 15:12-17: "My command is this: Love each other as I have loved you. Greater love has no one than this, that he lay down his life for his friends. You are my friends if you do what I command. I no longer call you servants, because a servant does not know his master's business. Instead, I have called you friends, for everything that I learned from my Father I have made known to you. You did not choose me, but I chose you and appointed you to go and bear fruit - fruit that will last. Then the Father will give you whatever you ask in my name. This is my command: Love each other."

We must understand that reclaiming our identity in Christ doesn't happen overnight, and there isn't a magic wand that I wave to set you right side up again. It's a commitment. It's a choice. It's putting your feet on the path and saying, "I refuse to let the enemy steal one more day!" There are no shortcuts in this journey. God is willing to take you back to the beginning to understand His original design and help you understand your past so you can move forward with everything He has in store. Keep taking one step at a time -holding His hand.

Baby Step 1

Here's where it's time to get off the edge of the bed. Here's where we take another step forward and tackle that list that you've had covering your heart. It's time to take off the sticky notes, one by one. Let them all go. You are NOT what the world says you are. You are not who the devil says you are. You don't have to stay where you are anymore. It's time to step into everything that God has in store for you and receive His identity. The one He has had for you all along. Write down the labels that have been defining you. It's time to bring them out into God's light.

_____

_____

_____

_____

_____

_____

_____

_____

_____

Baby Step 2

Look again at the list of labels on your list. Ask God to heal you as only He can do; to touch your heart, to whisper in your ear the loving words that you need to hear today.

Dear God,

Baby Step 3

Today, read Psalm 139:13-18. Meditate on these verses. Let them soak into the driest places of your heart. Let them nourish your soul. You are not defined by who the world says you are but by God. He made you. He formed you. He loves you.

Take a few moments and write out those verses below. Be intentional. Claim them as your truth, as accurate as writing your name.

Baby Step 4

Today, read Ephesians Chapter 1. As you read the beginning, add your name to the list of people Paul is addressing. Read this chapter as though he is speaking directly to you. Answer the following questions:

1. What were you predestined for? _____

2. In Jesus, what do you have? _____
_____

3. What mystery has He made known to you? _____

4. When you believe, what are you marked with? _____

5. What is that guaranteeing you? _____
_____

Meditate on these verses. Let the hope of these words strengthen and equip you for this journey. Claim these truths for yourself!

Baby Step 5

Today, read the verses below that remind you who you are in Christ!

"Yet to all who did receive him, to those who believed in his name, he gave the right to become children of God." ~ John 1:12

"In him we have redemption through his blood, the forgiveness of sins, in accordance with the riches of God's grace." ~ Ephesians 1:7

"You did not choose me, but I chose you and appointed you so that you might go and bear fruit - fruit that will last - and so that whatever you ask in my name the Father will give you." ~ John 15:16

"For we are god's handiwork, created in Christ Jesus to do good works, which God prepared in advance for us to do." ~ Ephesians 2:10

"But our citizenship is in heaven. And we eagerly await a Savior from there, the Lord Jesus Christ." ~ Philippians 3:20

Baby Step 6

So my question for you today is, are you ready? Are you going to believe God's Truth and choose to no longer wear the sticky notes of this world? Will you choose to believe that you were bought at a price and loved so much that God sacrificed His only Son on a cross? Are you ready to step out of the darkness and into His glorious light? If so, it's time to decree and declare what you now believe. Then sign your name.

Father God,

I know I'm a sinner, and I ask for Your forgiveness. I believe Jesus Christ is Your Son. I believe that he died for my sins and that You raised Him to life. I believe that the Holy Spirit is my helper and that He lives inside me. I believe in Your Word and that I need to renew my mind with it every day. I believe that I am created in Your image and that You love me. I want to trust Jesus as my Savior and follow Him every day from this day forward. Please guide my life and help me to do Your will. I pray this in the glorious name of Jesus. Amen

Signed: _____

Baby Step 7

Over the last seven days, what truth has been revealed to you? Do you have a better understanding of your identity and how you need to reclaim it? Use the journal space below to write out some new truths and what God has shown you.

Step 4

How Do I Keep My Identity? - Understanding Dominion And Authority

There have been times in my life where I've been presented with a solution for a problem, and I said to myself, "Oh, if it was only that easy." If I took this pill before eating, I was guaranteed to lose five pounds. If I used this hair product, I was assured that I would no longer have frizzy hair. If I bought these shoes, my back would have more support, and the world would be a brighter place. And while those solutions may not have worked that easily, there has been one solution given to me that has worked, and I want to share it with you today.

We often forget who we are when we forget what we already have, which brings me to the next step in our journey: understanding our dominion and authority. Now, if you are unclear about what those words mean, let's start there. Dominion means to rule over. It means jurisdiction, control, supremacy. Authority means power, influence, license. Now I love that word license. License means you have been given authority by someone else. Someone has issued you a license to do something.

I was in real estate for over 12 years, and I had a license to sell real estate. I would carry this card around with me, and it gave me the jurisdiction and power to buy and sell a property and it was issued to me by the State of

Michigan. I knew what I could do, and I was confident in that title of Realtor.

Now that you understand dominion and authority better, did you know that God gave us these things? And if you did know, do you feel like you are operating in His dominion and authority today? I bet if I could look through these pages, you wouldn't be raising your hand. I think there might be some more accurate words to describe how we are operating today in this world:

- powerless
- inferior
- lack
- weakness
- submissive
- helpless

So, how have we been living? I know for me, before I grabbed onto these truths and watched others I have journeyed with, you feel powerless. You move through the day absorbing every bit of discouragement, shock wave, piece of negative news, and illness, and you say, "I guess this is God's will for me. He must want me to go through this. He must want to teach me something." And before long, you start resenting God because you're thinking, I really can't take much more of this. If there is a lesson here, I want Him to move on and teach someone else. And in thinking this way, feeling discouraged, blaming God, wanting to give up, guess what? The enemy is winning because we've forgotten who we are.

If you know my story, you'll know that this was my life for seventeen years: feeling trapped, powerless, believing every lie, and blaming God. So I have a passion for this; it's part of my calling - to teach God's Word. Because I know what it feels like to lose my identity and authority in Christ. But friends, I also know how it feels to get it back, and I want you to experience that too.

So where in God's Word does it say that we have dominion and authority? Well, let's go back to the beginning and see what God told Adam and inturn is telling us:

Genesis 1:26-28 NKJV
"Then God said, 'Let us make man in our image, according to our likeness; let them have dominion over the fish of the sea, over the birds of the air, and over the cattle, over all the earth and over every creeping thing that creeps on the earth. So God created man in His own image in the image of God He created him; male and female He created them. Then God blessed them and said to them 'Be fruitful and multiply; fill the earth and subdue it; have dominion over the fish of the sea, over the birds of the air, and over every living thing that moves on the earth."

Did you read those words: Dominion. Subdue. God has given us the earth. It is our domain. And yet, the enemy of our soul has fallen here (yes, he was kicked out of heaven) and has taken over our territory and is working tirelessly to make us forget that it is our domain. Think about *that* for a second.

Let's talk about authority. Ultimately when we think of authority, we think of Jesus.

Matthew 28:18-20 NKJV
"And Jesus came and spoke to them saying 'All authority has been given to me in heaven and on earth."

And here's where the license comes in -

"Go therefore and make disciples of all the nations, baptizing them in the name of the Father and of the Son and of the Holy Spirit, teaching them to observe all things that I have commanded you; and lo, I am with you always, even to the end of the age."

Jesus is not just talking to the disciples here. He is not just talking to the pastors, ministers, priests, chaplains, youth group leaders, elders, and deacons. He is talking to the church. His body of believers. You and me. We all have a responsibility to do, teach and observe all the things that we have been commanded.

God gave Jesus this authority, Jesus gives us this authority, this license, so that while we are living here on this earth, where we have been given dominion, we may live in His promises and grow and further His Kingdom. In our identity in Christ.

But that's not what we see in today's world, do we? We've given up. We've taken our license and handed it over to the devil. He's come into our world and said, "Hey, I like it here. I think I'm going to make this my home and do whatever I want here. I'm going to wreak havoc on this world and make everyone forget who they are, what they believe, and who is the true King."
I don't know about you, but I'm tired of that thinking. I've taken back my license. Are you ready to take back your's too?

Kenneth Hagin, a great man of God who is no longer with us, writes this: "Everything has been placed under Jesus' feet (Ephesians 1:22). That includes the devil. Since we are part of the Body of Christ, all things are under our feet as well. That means the devil is under our feet as well."

If we can remember God's Word, if we can tuck it away and stand on its truth as our solid foundation, it won't matter what problem comes against us. It won't matter what the enemy is attempting to do in our lives. It won't matter what scheme he comes at us with, whether physical, emotional, or financial. We can walk on top of every one of these situations and remember that no weapon formed against us shall prosper. He is under our feet. We have the victory.

My friends, isn't it time to take back our dominion and authority? It's how we will keep our identity while living in this broken world. It's time to remember who we are and whose we are - sons and daughters of the Highest King. Amen.

Baby Step 1

How would you describe your current life situation? Do you feel that you have the dominion and authority that is given to us by Jesus Christ? Do you feel like you can do anything because of who is living in you?

Baby Step 2

Look again at the words you used to describe your current situation. We have to remember that feelings and emotions can change from day to day, but our God never changes. Use the space below to tell Him how you are feeling right now and invite Him into your life to work and move.

Dear God,

Baby Step 3

Today, read Ephesians 1:17-23. Meditate on the hope that Paul is giving us. Answer the following questions below.

1. What does Paul keep asking God for ? _____

2. What are we promised when the eyes of our heart are opened?
_____
_____

3. What power is Paul talking about ? _____

4. What things are placed under Jesus' feet? _____

5. What is subject to the name of Jesus? _____
_____

Meditate on these verses. Let the hope of these words strengthen and equip you for this journey. Claim these truths for yourself!

Baby Step 4

Today, re-read Ephesians Chapter 1:17-23. We cannot reclaim our identity and with that our dominion and authority until we know without a doubt that everything is subject to the name of Jesus. And - that we can send everything the enemy tries to give us to His feet. Read below where we can have victory in our lives.

- Because of Jesus, we can take dominion in our homes. Our home can be a sanctuary for God's presence. A place of peace for you and your family. What would it be like to have the world fall away as you walked through the door and live in the constant peace of God?
- Because of Jesus, we can have victory over sin. We don't have to live with our past mistakes and regret. We don't have to keep recycling the lies from the enemy and wearing the labels given to us by the broken people we have encountered.
- Because of Jesus, we can have victory over disease. Today is the day that you say, "I will not receive one more thing from the enemy. In Christ, I am a new creation. I walk in divine health. I cast every illness, every diagnosis to the feet of Jesus and claim His truth. By His stripes, I am healed."
- Because of Jesus, we can live victorious, triumphant lives in Him. And it begins today.

Baby Step 5

What does it mean to live a life with dominion and authority?

I use to think that being a Christian and loving God meant that I would never encounter struggles. I've heard from many others that they, too, believed this way, and when they experienced pain and suffering, they believed it was God's will. But with that acceptance also the question, "Why does God want me to suffer?"

This way of thinking couldn't be further from the truth. The Bible is clear that being a follower of Jesus will not be easy. In Matthew 16:24, Jesus tells His disciples, "If anyone would come after me, let him deny himself and take up his cross and follow me." Taking up our cross is what Jesus did. It's dying to self daily. It's trusting and following. It's being obedient and not only reading God's Word but doing what it says.

But these aren't the struggles I am referring to. We have to remember that we are fighting an enemy, that this is a battle, and what the enemy is throwing at us each day is designed to make us forget who we are. He has come to steal, kill and destroy; steal our joy, our health, and our families. But when we know who we are and who is living inside us and everything is under Jesus' feet, the devil may try, but he won't succeed because He who is in us is GREATER than he who is in the world. That is what we have to remember. That is what we stand on. That is our truth!

Baby Step 6

So now that we understand our dominion and authority, it's time to take it back. Use the prayer below. Stand in your home, say the prayer out loud, and believe its words. It's time to establish our dominion and authority where we live AND live it out each day. Are you ready?

Father God,
We thank you that You gave us dominion over the earth. And even though sin entered the world, Jesus, who died as a sinless man, re-established that dominion, and we claim that today! We ask that You cover this domain by the blood of Jesus and put a boundary around this place. We know that everything belongs to You, God, and that You have given everything to us. We thank you that we are joint-heirs with Jesus Christ and that we are in covenant with You, God. We thank you that all that we have is Yours and that all that You have is ours.
We stand here, open-handed, in covenant with You, and we re-establish Your order and dominion and say right now that everything that is not of God has to go in Jesus' name. We are declaring, devil, that this is our domain, and we take authority over this home. Anything that was done here or said here is null and void and has to go. This is now a place of peace, joy, and healing. This home is now a sanctuary for the presence of God, and we will keep it that way. We will keep our eye gates, ear gates, and mouth gates pure. And we say all of these things in Jesus' name. Amen

Baby Step 7

Over the last seven days, what truth has been revealed to you? Do you have a better understanding of your dominion and authority? Use the journal space below to write out some new truths and what God has shown you.

Step 5

How Do I Fight? - Putting On The Full Armor Of God

If I look back to the darkest moments in my life, I wanted to give up. I didn't have the strength in me to keep putting one foot in front of the other and meeting life head-on. I wanted to stay under the covers. I tried to sleep the day away. I wanted to be alone in my sadness.

As I've talked with others throughout my life, they have experienced the exact same thing. They wanted to pull away. They wanted to be alone. They contemplated ending their life and believed that would be the best for everyone. As I sit here today, looking at both sides of my journey - it's easy to see the battle I was in. It's easy to see where the enemy was encouraging me to give up. It's easy to see why I wasn't winning. But at the moment, all I could see was the lies, and the last thing I wanted to do was fight.

Maybe you're right where I was years ago. Perhaps you feel like all you've done is fight, and you have no strength left. Maybe you've never even recognized it was a battle and have just been receiving every blow from the enemy like it's the most normal thing to do. Well, as we take this next step in our journey, we are going to recognize that this is a battle, that we can't do it in our strength, and that the bible gives us precisely what we need to fight.

If we want to know about the battle we're facing, we need to go to God's Word. We read in Ephesians 6:10-18 that the battle is real. We face an enemy we cannot see and fight a battle, not with physical weapons but with spiritual ones. And when we don't even realize it's a battle, we move through our lives day in and day out struggling - listening to lie after lie, believing that we are anything but the sons and daughters that God created us to be. One day, we wake up to find that our identities have been stolen, our families divided, and our health is hanging in the balance. It's as though we were struck in the night, we're injured and bleeding, and our adversary - the devil - has walked off with all the spoils.

Ephesians 6:12 uses the word "struggle" in the NIV translation. But if you use the King James Version, the word is "wrestle." We have to remember that Paul was writing this to the readers of his time. They knew what it was to wrestle. During this period, men competed during the Greek Olympics and various festivals. They understood the logistics of wrestling:

- Always face your opponent.
- Never turn your back.
- Stay alert. One sudden move could catch you off guard.
- You never lose physical contact. It's face-to-face, hand-to-hand combat.

The reader of this time would have witnessed this sport and put into perspective what it's like to battle the enemy. They would have understood that we are fighting for our very lives and need to be ready for combat. We need to say alert and can never turn our back on his attempts and what he is trying to accomplish.

And what are the devil's goals? His greatest desire has always been to push us out of fellowship with God. He does that by lying to us, isolating us, and distracting us until we want to give up. He hates that we are created in God's image and that God sent Jesus to the earth to demolish the enemy's plans. He's not creative but consistent and uses strategies against us to wear us down at every turn. When he was kicked out of heaven, his angels came with him. We read in Revelation 12:9: "And the great dragon was thrown down, that ancient serpent, who is called the devil and Satan, the deceiver of the whole world - he was thrown down to the earth, and his angels were thrown down with him."

These verses tell us that we're not just fighting the devil, but his many minions: the spirit of confusion, the spirit of addiction, the spirit of infirmity, the spirit of depression, the spirit of suicide, the spirit of anger, the familiar spirit, the spirit of jealousy, the lying spirit, the spirit of bondage, and the spirit of fear- just to name a few.

And while we're so busy bumping along in our lives, unaware of the battle, and fighting each step of the way against the enemy, we're losing pieces of ourselves. We forget who we are, the power we have inside of us because of Jesus, and how the enemy is under our feet.

You see, the devil knows who we are. He knows what we're capable of. And he knows he loses his effect when we wake up, rise up, and put on the full armor of God. So he relentlessly lies and tries and strategizes against us until we forget, feel like we are without hope, and want to give up.

Are you able to see where the enemy has been working and strategizing in your life to distract you from God? Priscilla Shirer, the author of *The Armor of God*, points out the enemy's strategies to attack. Take a look below and see whether you can recognize some of the ways in which the enemy has been attacking you.

Strategy #1 - Against Your Passion
He seeks to dim your whole desire for prayer, dull your interest in spiritual things, and downplay the potency of your most strategic weapons (Ephesians 6:10-20).

Strategy #2 - Against Your Focus
He disguises himself and manipulates your perspective so you end up focusing on the wrong culprit, directing your weapons at the wrong enemy (2 Corinthians 11:14).

Strategy #3 - Against Your Identity
He magnifies your insecurities, leading you to doubt what God says about you to disregard what He has given you (Ephesians 1:17 -19).

Strategy #4 - Against Your Family
He wants to disintegrate your family, dividing your home and rendering it chaotic, restless, and unfruitful (Genesis 3:1-7).

Strategy #5 - Against Your Confidence

He constantly reminds you of your past mistakes and bad choices, hoping to convince you that you're under God's judgment rather than under the blood (Revelation 12:10).

Strategy #6 - Against Your Calling

He amplifies fear, worry, and anxiety until they're the loudest voices in your head, causing you to deem the adventure of following God too risky to attempt (Joshua 14:8).

Strategy #7 - Against Your Purity

He tries to tempt you toward certain sins, convincing you that you can tolerate them without risking consequences, knowing that they'll only wedge distance between yourself and God (Isaiah 59:1-2).

Strategy #8 - Against Your Rest and Contentment

He hopes to overload your life and schedule, pressuring you to constantly push beyond your limits, never feeling permission to say no (Deuteronomy 5:15).

Strategy #9 - Against Your Heart

He uses every opportunity to keep old wounds fresh in your mind, knowing that anger and hurt and bitterness and unforgiveness will continue to roll the damage forward (Hebrews 12:15).

Strategy #10 - Against Your Relationships
He creates disruption and disunity within your circle of friends and within the shared community of the body of Christ (1 Timothy 2:8).

    If you're like me, you can read each one of those strategies and know that you've been at war with the enemy. But what I love about God is that He doesn't leave us unprepared. He has given us armor. And not any armor, His armor - to put on each day and fight. Just like everything else, we have to choose to get up off that couch, climb out from under the covers, step out from our discouragement and sadness and admit we're in this battle and that we can't do it in our strength anymore. It's time, my friends, to put on the full armor of God and fight.

    Over the next seven days, we're going to step into that full armor. It's time to understand each piece, why it's essential, and most importantly, put it on!

Baby Step 1

We may not understand all the pieces yet, but it's time to get into practice putting it on. Use the diagram below to help you put on the full armor of God. Say the words out loud, putting on each piece. Begin today.

HELMET — I will put on the helmet of Salvation to protect my head. I will not listen to the lies of the enemy and only believe God's Truth.

BREAST PLATE — I will put on the breastplate of righteousness, which covers my heart and other vital organs. It protects against Satan's accusations. I will guard my heart.

BELT OF TRUTH — I will put on the belt of truth, which holds all the other pieces in place. I will believe in God's scriptural truth and not the lies of the enemy.

SHOES OF THE GOSPEL — I will put on the shoes of the gospel, grounding myself in the gospel of peace.

SHIELD OF FAITH — I will pick up the shield of faith, which extinguishes all the flaming arrows of the evil one. And I commit that I will grow my faith and this shield.

SWORD OF THE SPIRIT — I will pick up the sword of the spirit, which is God's Word and fight against the enemy.

Baby Step 2

Let's take a few moments and understand where you are at in the battle. Ask yourself the questions below and answer honestly. Allow God to show you what changes you need to make and where you have been wrestling with the enemy.

1. Do you now see that you are in a spiritual battle ? _____

2. What strategies has the enemy been using against you?
   _____
   _____

3. Do you struggle with reading God's Word? _____

4. Think of some ways you can dig deeper into God's Truth each day?
   _____

5. Are you ready to put on the full armor of God and fight? Explain why.
   _____
   _____

Baby Step 3

Today, let's understand the **belt of truth**, the **breastplate of righteousness**, and the **shoes of the gospel of peace**.

The Belt of Truth
Why is the belt of truth so important? Because it holds all of the other pieces in place. We need to understand scriptural truth, as opposed to the lies of the enemy. We need to stand firm on a solid foundation - the truth based on God's Word. We need to remember that we are loved, that we are forgiven, and that we have hope in Jesus Christ.

The Breastplate of Righteousness
When we put on the breastplate of righteousness, it covers our heart and guards it, along with all our other vital organs. It also protects us against all of Satan's accusations. The Bible says, "Above all else, guard your heart, for everything you do flows from it" (Proverbs 4:23). The breastplate is not comprised of our righteousness because the Bible is clear that none of us is righteous in ourselves (Romans 3:10). It is made up of Christ's righteousness, which He gives us freely when we accept Him as our Savior.

Shoes of the Gospel of Peace
What are you wearing today that centers your disposition on peace? These shoes that we put on center us for the day. When we have the peace of Jesus, we can speak peace into our families, situations, and communities. The enemy will not persuade us to react. We will walk in comfort, confidence, and continuity. We will walk in peace.

Baby Step 4

Today, let's understand the **shield of faith**, the **helmet of salvation**, and the **sword of the spirit**.

The Shield of Faith

Paul writes in Romans 12:3 that God gifts each of us a measure of faith. To repeat, in case you missed it, faith is a gift. We then need to grow our faith by fellowshipping with the Lord and spending time in His Word until our measure grows and develops. We can then pick up this shield and block the devil's fiery darts of doubt, his tempting list of lies, and live a victorious life, confident of who we are and whose we are.

The Helmet of Salvation

When we put on the helmet, it protects our head, perhaps the most vital part of our body. Our brain is the organ with which we think and process, and dream. We need to protect our thoughts and not allow the enemy to penetrate our minds. We need to be confident of our truth and certain that our foundation is rooted and based on the Word of God.

The Sword of the Spirit

While all the other armor of God is defensive in nature, the sword of the Spirit is the weapon used for offense. Hebrews 4:12 describes God's Word as "alive and active. Sharper than any double-edged sword." It was Jesus himself who showed us how to pick up this sword and fight against the enemy. While He was tempted for forty days and forty nights in the desert, he fought the enemy by using this very sword: "It is written... (e.g., Matthew 4:4). God's Truth is powerful and will not only protect us from our enemy, the devil, but will help us fight when he tempts us.

Paul closes by saying, "And pray in the Spirit on all occasions with all kinds of prayers and requests. With this in mind, be alert and always keep on praying for all the Lord's people" (Ephesians 6:18). It's not enough to just put on the full armor of God every day; we need to cover it all with prayer. This can be prayers that we say over ourselves or when we join our brothers and sisters in Christ and go to war with them.

Baby Step 5

Today, read Matthew 4:1-11, then read the observations below.

When we read these verses about Jesus being tempted in the wilderness, there is so much we can learn about our own battles with the enemy:

- First, we need to recognize that if Jesus was tempted, we will be also. It may not be a face-to-face encounter like Jesus had, but we are reminded in God's Word that our struggle is not against flesh and blood but against the spiritual forces of evil. So each day, we need to put on our armor and fight.

- Second, how does Jesus fight back? With God's Word. "It is Written" was used each time the enemy came at Him, and each time Jesus put him in his place.

- Thirdly, Jesus gives us the very words we need to use: "Away from me, Satan!" We have the power, in Jesus' name, to rebuke the enemy and send him running. We just have to be mindful and do it.

Everywhere you look today, the enemy is wreaking havoc and fighting against us. We need to reclaim our authority in Christ and fight back. Use God's Word as your weapon, put on the full armor of God, and fight back!

Baby Step 6

Sometimes it can appear overwhelming to open our eyes and see another world. Yesterday it was just us, trying to live our lives, and today we realize that we are fighting an invisible war and are told to put on the full armor of God. But can you see that Jesus is leading us out of Egypt and away from slavery? He is even orchestrating our way out of the desert, and now we're standing at the edge of Jordan, looking at the life that could be ours. We could stay in the desert, continuing to believe the lies and not living to our full potential in Christ. Or we could keep moving forward, into all the promises God has in store for us and into the kind of life we can only have with Him. We have a choice. What will you choose?

Father God,
Thank you for opening my eyes. Thank you for allowing me to see this battle and for giving me the tools with which to fight. Help me put on the full armor of God every day and to bathe all of the components in prayer. I lift up myself, my family, neighbors, and those I do not know and pray for Your strength and truth. Thank you that You have already won this war! Thank you that You died on the cross to save me from my sins, and You have conquered death. I love You. I praise You. I ask all of these things in your precious name. Amen

Baby Step 7

Over the last seven days, what truth has been revealed to you? Do you have a better understanding of the full armor of God? Use the journal space below to write out some new truths and what God has shown you.

Step 6

Grace Over Guilt - You Can Always Return To The Path

In 2017, I had the opportunity to go to Israel. It was a once-in-a-lifetime trip, where you literally walked where Jesus walked. We were led each day by our teacher and learned to follow. We had to follow directions, follow where he led, and follow the journey that the Lord took each of us on.

There were so many things I didn't know. I had spent seventeen years walking around with my head down, listening to the lies of the enemy, believing that God had forgotten me. When I think about this trip, God brought me all the way to this precious land so that I could return. I needed to return to His original design. I needed to return to who He was calling me to be. I needed to return to the path.

How did He do this? The same way Jesus did when He was teaching the disciples. The more challenging the hike, the more significant the teachings. And we hiked all over Israel. We started at the top of the Makhtesh Ramon and climbed down to the flat part of the Negev. We went to Azekah, where David killed Goliath and had tea in a Bedouin tent in Hebron. We went to Capernaum, where Jesus did so much of His teaching and did mikveh, or ceremonial washing, in the Jordan River. We climbed Mt. Gilboa, where King Saul died, and did the precipitous climb to the top of Mt. Arbel, where Jesus is said to have commissioned his disciples (Matthew 28:16-20.) We were told that it was up this mountain, overlooking their whole world, that Jesus would have wanted them to go. Through all of this, I pushed myself past any point I had ever gone before.

We went to Jerusalem and prayed at the Wailing Wall, and I stood in the Garden of Gethsemane, where Jesus prayed the night before he would be crucified. I did many other things, making the experience as real to me as I now saw God.

And each step of the journey, I learned more and more. I learned that whenever God calls, you listen; you need to awaken your ability to trust and let down your walls and know that you are stronger with God's help. Listen to the Rabbi, heed the disciple's calling, and earnestly set your feet upon the path. To take in God's Word and exhale the old way of life. Exalt the Lord for the perfect fabric He has woven in you and take the message to the nations.

At one point in the journey, we took our socks and shoes off. We stood on the path, letting our feet get acclimated to the terrain. We started out walking slowly, stepping deliberately, being aware of each step. As we chatted, there was a low hum of noise, feeling the difference between the hiking boots we were using and now our bare feet. Then the teacher's voice filled the air: "This is what it's like when we roll our path onto God's."

It made perfect sense. The hiking boots I was wearing were like the confidence I had in myself. I could go wherever I wanted. At whatever speed I wanted. I could choose the path I wanted to go. But when I stood there, sockless and shoeless, I needed to go slowly and deliberately. I needed to rely on God. I was rolling my life and my path onto the Lord's.

When I came home from Israel, I was a changed person. I read the Bible differently, worshipped differently, looked at myself differently. I traveled less and less without shoes and socks, taking the path slowly and deliberately. God continued to reinforce in me that the battle we face each day is a spiritual one. That the devil is constantly trying to distract us and detour us from God's truth but that God's made a way for us to be victorious. And His name is Jesus!

Romans 6:1-6 asks us some introspective heart questions: "What shall we say then? Shall we continue in sin that grace may abound? Certainly not? How shall we who died to sin live any longer in it. Or do you not know that as many of us were baptized into Christ Jesus were baptized into His death? Therefore we were buried with Him through baptism into death, that just as Christ was raised from the dead, by the glory of the Father, even so we also should walk in newness of life. For if we have been united together in the likeness of His death, certainly we also shall be in the likeness of His resurrection, knowing this, that our old man was crucified with Him (old nature, our flesh) that the body of sin might be done away with, that we should no longer be slaves to sin."

And isn't that the question? Why are we still slaves to sin, guilt, and shame when we know what Jesus did for us on the cross? Why are we walking around, receiving every lie from the enemy, hanging onto our past, when we could be free?

Part of the problem is that our "stuff" is familiar. We get used to the guilt and shame and would rather hang onto what we know than step out into what we cannot see like trusting God. We see this in Exodus when we read about the Israelites. While they were following God, they said, "Take us back to Egypt!" They were complaining about food and water and would have instead gone back to Egypt, even though they were slaves, then step out each day and trust in the Lord.

Trusting God can be uncomfortable. Our flesh isn't being fed with those familiar things like when we're in control. Like when we're wearing our socks and hiking boots and able to go wherever we choose. And the enemy will undoubtedly try and distract us, making us believe that we don't need God and can do it ourselves. Because even the devil knows we can't.

But we have to remember that when Jesus is living inside of us, we have the authority. We have the power. We have His grace. But we have to let go of the things of this world and hang onto Jesus. We have to roll our lives onto His path. We have to return. And we always can.

Oswald Chamber writes this in his book My Utmost for His Highest, "Even the weakest saint can experience the power of the deity of the Son of God, when he is willing to 'let go.' But any effort to 'hang on' to the least bit of our own power will only diminish the life of Jesus in us. We have to keep letting go, and slowly, but surely, the great full life of God will invade us, penetrating every part. Then Jesus will have complete and effective dominion in us, and people will take notice that we have been with Him."

So how do we return to the path? We choose. And it's a daily choice. Each morning when we open our eyes and drop our feet to the floor, we have to choose whether we're going to throw on those socks and hiking boots or whether we'll stay barefoot. We have to keep letting go, letting go of the familiar, letting go of the guilt, letting go of the past. Before long, it will hardly be an effort to let go of what's in your hand and to reach out and grab the hand of Jesus. "Where do you want to go today, Lord? I'm ready!"

We also need to remember that one of the biggest reasons we struggle is when we try and do things in our own strength and power. We need to remember that we need Jesus! He gives us the license. It's His power and strength in us that help us be overcomers and live triumphantly, even in a broken world. We can't do it without Him, so we need to stop trying.

And finally, we need to remember that when we actively pursue Jesus in our daily lives, people will take notice. People will see Jesus in us. This allows us the opportunity to share the Gospel and how Jesus is working in our lives. By your testimony. This is what grows the Kingdom of God! And as we reclaim our identity in Christ, we will be helping our families, friends, and community reclaim theirs.

On May 20th, 2017, while taking one of the most incredible adventures with God in Israel, I wrote this note to Him: "You are an awesome God! You invited me here, helped me pay, made the way, and now I see and know so much more than I imagined. Please forgive me for just seeing one side of You when You are like a diamond. Please help me roll my life onto Your path, walk slowly and deliberately, and do Your will. Help me to be your disciple and to Halak - walk the text. I love you, Lord, Ammie."

Are you ready to receive His grace? Are you prepared to return to the path? It's time to take off those socks and shoes. It's time to roll your life onto the Lord's.

Baby Step 1

Today I want you to focus your attention on the word "choose." Choose to be intentional. Choose to believe and receive the grace that Jesus so freely offers us. Choose to return to the path.

Baby Step 2

Today, read Psalm 16. Meditate on these verses. This is David's prayer to the Lord, declaring his trust and reliance on Him. If you could write a prayer to the Lord today, what would you say?

Dear God,

Baby Step 3

Are you still wondering how to roll your life onto the Lord's, to return to the path? Today, read Proverbs 3:5-6. This is one of my favorite proverbs. Notice that it begins with action and ends with a promise. Claim this truth and these promises for yourself.

Proverbs 3:5-6

"Trust in the LORD with all your heart
and lean not on your own understanding; in all your ways
submit to him, and he will make your paths straight." ~ Proverbs 3:5-6

First - Trust in the Lord with all my heart.

Second - Admit, right now, that I'm not capable of making good decisions, and I don't understand what's going on. But I'm not going to react; I'm going to rest.

Third - With everything that I am, I will cry out to God. I will pray to Him and praise His name.

The Promise - He will direct my path.

Remember, God's WORD is where we need to go for our truth. He will make our paths straight!

Baby Step 4

Today, read the excerpt below from Joni Eareckson Tada's book: *A Step Further.*

"The Bible tells us our God is so trustworthy that we are to throw our confidence on Him, not leaning on our own understanding (Proverbs 3:5). God has already proved how much His love and be trusted by sending Christ to die for us. Wasn't that enough? Not for me. I always wanted to be on the inside looking out - sitting with Lord up in the control tower instead of down on the confusing ground level. He couldn't be trusted unless I was there to oversee things! What a low view of my Master and Creator I had held all these years!

How could I have dared to assume that almighty God owed me explanations! Did I think that because I had done God the 'favor' of becoming a Christian, He must now check things out with me? Was the Lord of the universe under obligation to show me how the trials of every human being fit into the tapestry of life? Had I never read Deuteronomy 29:29, 'There are secrets of the Lord your God has not revealed to us' (LB)?

What made me think that even if He explained all His ways to me I would be able to understand them? It would be like pouring million-gallon truths into my one-ounce brain."

Baby Step 5

Today, read the excerpt below from Mary Fairchild as she writes about God's Grace.

"The doctrine of grace stands at the center of the Bible. It is the theme that connects every book and the thread that winds through every verse. In the original Old Testament language, *grace* comes from a word meaning 'lovingkindness,' which is often used to describe the Lord's character. God's grace flows from the essence of his being. "The LORD, the LORD, a God merciful and gracious, slow to anger, and abounding in steadfast love and faithfulness" (Exodus 34:6 ESV).

In the New Testament, *grace* is translated from a term meaning 'divine favor,' 'goodwill,' 'that which gives joy,' and 'that which is a free gift.' Grace is the undeserved gift of God. The greatest of God's gifts of grace is His Son, Jesus Christ.

The simple acronym is frequently cited as a biblical definition of grace: **G**od's **R**iches **A**t **C**hrist's **E**xpense.

The Bible tells us that God's grace is manifested in the person of Jesus Christ. 'The Word became flesh and made his dwelling among us. We have seen his glory, the glory of the one and only Son, who came from the Father, full of grace and truth...Out of his fullness we have all received grace in place of grace already given. For the law was given through Moses; grace and truth came through Jesus Christ" (John 1:14-17, NIV).

By God's grace, sinners are saved and reborn into the family of God. God offers eternal life to all who believe in His son, Jesus. Through Christ's substitutionary death on the cross, God pronounces 'not guilty' all who repent, confess their sins, and believe in Jesus Christ as their Lord and Savior. As sinners, we deserve to die in our sins, but God's grace gives us everlasting life through Jesus Christ."

Baby Step 6

Today, read the verses below about God's grace. Let it be a reminder that we can have grace over guilt, and that we can return to His path.

"Who saved us and called us to a holy calling, not because of our works but because of his own purpose and grace, which he gave us in Christ Jesus before the ages began." ~ 2 Timothy 1:9

"The Word became flesh and made his dwelling among us. We have seen his glory, the glory of the one and only Son, who came from the Father, full of grace and truth." ~ John 1:14

"In him we have redemption through his blood, the forgiveness of sins, in accordance with the riches of God's grace." ~ Ephesians 1:7

"But he said to me, 'My grace is sufficient for you, for my power is made perfect in weakness.' Therefore I will boast all the more gladly of my weaknesses, so that the power of Christ may rest upon me." ~ 2 Corinthians 12:9

"Let us then approach the throne of grace with confidence, so that we may receive mercy and find grace to help us in our time of need." ~ Hebrews 4:16

Baby Step 7

Over the last seven days, what truth has been revealed to you? Do you have a better understanding of God's grace? Are you ready to return to His path? Use the journal space below to write out some new truths and what God has shown you.

Step 7

Seed, Time, And Harvest - Growing in God

I had never given much thought to seed, time, and harvest. I wouldn't say I was born with a green thumb, but I definitely love digging in the dirt, and I've always had a great appreciation for watching the flowers come up and the wonderment of spring. But in 2020, the year of slowing down and re-evaluation, I had the opportunity to have my own garden, and I got to be a part of the whole experience.

Buying the seeds was like a mystery to read. There were different sizes, shapes, and colors. I wasn't sure who was going to do what, but I hoped that in the end, I would grow what was pictured on the outside of the envelope. But what amazed me was that everything inside that tiny seed contained what was needed for that carrot or cucumber or radish to grow.

I then realized it wasn't just about putting a seed in the ground and hoping for the best. I needed to dig up the leaves and the weeds from the season before. I needed to prepare the soil. I needed to press that little hole into the ground and carefully plant one seed, keeping enough distance so it could grow properly. And I needed to keep the garden watered. And if all of these things weren't enough - then I needed to wait. I decided early on that checking for growth probably wouldn't happen in the first two days. But it didn't happen in the next two either. It was going to take time, and I would need to be patient.

And while I waited, I trusted and believed that what I had planted would grow. And it did. One afternoon I walked out to the garden and was filled with joy. Tiny, green shoots peppered the dirt. After that, it seemed that they visibly grew each day. And as I watched, I would say, "Okay, this is it. They must be ready now." But then something would happen, and a flower would appear, or another leaf grew. More waiting. More time. More changes.

But eventually, after the summer months rolled on and after the perfect amount of time had passed, the vegetables in the garden were ready, and it was time to harvest. I'm not sure I ever tasted a tomato like the ones I grew. So good!

Seed. Time. Harvest. This experience with the garden opened up my mind to new teachings. And I discovered that everything is about seed, time, and harvest and that every Word of God is a seed. We read in John 1:1-3: "In the beginning was the Word, and the Word was with God, and the Word was God. He was with God in the beginning. Through him all things were made; without him nothing was made that has been made."

Jesus came into the world as the Word. As the seed. A seed sown into the world. And why did God send Jesus? He came to restore the world, cancel the enemy's plans, give life, and give it abundantly. Psalm 107:20 says: "He sent out His word and healed them, he rescued them from the grave."

My friends, Jesus is the seed. He represents the promise of new life, forgiveness of sins, broken chains, restored relationships, and death to sin. The devil, our enemy, tried to stop that seed. He thought he was finally winning by crucifying God's son and watching Him hang on a cross. But God!

God planted that seed in the ground, and three days later, what came up changed everything! Jesus rose from the dead! Everything was new in the Spirit! The curtain in the temple was torn in two because we are no longer separated from God. Hallelujah!

So let's take a moment and apply seed, time, and harvest to our lives. What are we planting in the garden of our hearts? We now know that we are created in God's image and are not only made up of flesh but of Spirit. God spoke the world into existence, so we know there is power in the spoken Word. Are we planting peace, joy, and love? Or are we planting seeds of bitterness, anger, and resentment? God's Word tells us in Galatians 6:7-9, "Do not be deceived: God cannot be mocked. A man reaps what he sows. Whoever sows to please their flesh, from the flesh will reap destruction; whoever sows to please the Spirit, from the Spirit will reap eternal life. Let us not become weary in doing good, for at the proper time we will reap a harvest if we do not give up."

It's challenging to look at our lives when sometimes all we see are the weeds. But we forget that God is always moving, always working, planting, and anticipating the harvest. And He's willing to wait and be patient for that growth, to see the green sprouts peppering His earth. God was willing to sacrifice His only Son so that we could reap the benefits of eternal life. He's patiently waiting for you to roll your life onto His path, to remember who He created you to be and that He loves you with an everlasting love. He is the Master Gardener, and He wants you to keep growing in Him. That's right, keep growing. You've never stopped. God doesn't waste one ounce of pain that you've experienced, and He wants to grow something beautiful in your life.

It's also challenging because, in our flesh, we want to see those results now. Maybe you are in a season of hardship. Perhaps you are in a season of waiting. But I want to encourage you to believe in God's Word, believe in His promises, and allow Him to plant that seed in your life, and trust that in His timing, you will have a harvest without end. That's who God is, and that's how much He loves us.

How do we grow in God? We need to remember that this life is a journey and that when we someday close our eyes in this world, it's not the end. This isn't our permanent home. Ultimately the seeds that are being planted today in your life will be harvested in Heaven. And the enemy doesn't want you to remember this. He wants to continually distract you, detour you, and bring you out of fellowship with God. He wants to constantly lie to you so that you forget who you are in Christ. But no more. It's time to wake up. It's time to reclaim your identity before it's too late.

God has been patiently waiting, but the hour is drawing near. The earth is groaning for Jesus' return, and we can audibly hear the cries of its people. The enemy knows he only has a short time remaining, and he's wreaking as much havoc as possible before Jesus returns. Romans 13:11-14 says this: "And do this, understanding the present time: The hour has already come for you to wake up from your slumber, because our salvation is nearer now than when we first believed. The night is nearly over; the day is almost here. So let us put aside the deeds of darkness and put on the armor of light. Let us behave decently, as in the daytime, not in carousing and drunkenness, not in sexual immorality and debauchery, not in dissenter and jealousy. Rather, clothe yourselves with the Lord Jesus Christ, and do not think about how to gratify the desires of the flesh."

There's a reason this is the final, seventh step. Over the last seven weeks, God has been preparing the soil in your heart. He's been pulling the weeds of your past and helping you understand who you are in Christ. He's planted seeds of love, truth and given you the tools you need to fight against the enemy. He's shown you that His grace covers a multitude of sins and that there is nothing that can separate you from His love. He's invited you to return to His path and wants you to know that He's been working and moving in your life all this time. He wants to grow a beautiful garden of righteousness, joy, peace, love, and forgiveness in you. He wants the fruits of this garden to disburse to your family, your friends, your community, and the world. Are you ready? Seed, time, and harvest. It's time.

"Sow for yourselves righteousness; reap steadfast love; break up your fallow ground, for it is time to seek the Lord, that he may come and rain righteousness upon you."

Hosea 10:12

Baby Step 1

Today I want you to focus your attention on Matthew 6:33: "But seek first the kingdom of God and his righteousness, and all these things will be added to you." What would it look like to seek God first in your life? To trust in Him alone? To allow Him to work in the garden of your heart?

Baby Step 2

Today, spend some quiet time with God. Allow Him to show you where He needs to plant seeds of Truth. Ask Him to open up your heart so you can grow in the areas He shows you. Ask Him to help you see a particular situation through His eyes.

Dear God,

Baby Step 3

Today, read Luke 8:1-15, and answer the questions below.

1. Where are you planting your seeds? _____

2. What truth are you currently standing on?
   _____
   _____

3. Is God's Word feeding your heart or being choked out by life's worries and fears?
   _____

4. What is the key to this parable?
   _____

5. What does the "seed" represent in this story?
   _____
   _____

Baby Step 4

Today, read the excerpt below from Phillip Keller's book: *A Gardener Looks at the Fruits of the Spirit.*

"It is not good enough to 'half listen' to God. He demands my total concentration on what He is conveying to me. He knows that anything less will leave me half-hearted. My positive response results in immediate action on my part. His will is done. His wishes carried out. His desires are complied with happily. His commands are executed without delay or debate.

In short I simply do what He asks me to do. This is faith in action - the faith of obedience. This is the gateway into the good ground of God's garden. This is to 'hear' the Word and have it come alive. This is to have him implant the good seed of His good intentions for me in the good, warm, open, prepared soil of my responsive soul. The seed will germinate. The young plants will prosper and grow vigorously. There will be fruit production of His choosing - a harvest that delights Him and refreshes others."

Baby Step 5

My question for you today is, do you have difficulty waiting on God? During a season of waiting, what posture do you take? One of prayer? One of preparation? One of praise?

Waiting is hard. And it's easy to get ahead of ourselves and work on our agenda while we're waiting for God. We stand in the hallway, waiting for a door to open, and we say to ourselves, "I'll help God out. Then it will go a little faster." I've rationalized that before. But to honestly wait for Him, wait for Him to completely open that door in His timing, we have to be patient. We have to put our hope and trust in His promises. We have to praise Him while we're waiting.

I challenge you today that if you are waiting on something, stay true to God's timeline. He will give you the strength and the peace until He opens that door. And in the meantime, praise Him in the hallway.

"Do not be anxious about anything, but in every situation, by prayer and petition, with thanksgiving, present your requests to God. And the peace of God, which transcends all understanding, will guard your hearts and your minds in Christ Jesus."

Philippians 4:6-7

Baby Step 6

Today, read Psalm 34. These verses are filled with action. Write out some of the verbs that you find. What word is repeated over and over again? What do these verses say to your heart? Write out your answers below.

Baby Step 7

Over the last seven days, what truth has been revealed to you? Do you have a better understanding of God's grace? Are you ready to return to His path? Use the journal space below to write out some new truths and what God has shown you.

Closing Thoughts

As we turn on the news today, you can tangibly feel the brokenness of this world. Fear, discouragement, depression, and helplessness ooze out from our televisions and phones and stick to us unequivocally. We can feel the weight of the struggle in the spirit and mourn for our brothers and sisters who live in darkness. We could sit back and succumb. We could let each wave wash over us and take us further out to sea, forgetting who we are and where we're going. But do we really want to? Now that we know the truth, isn't it time to get up and fight?

If you look across the horizon, you can see Him coming! He's riding a white horse with eyes like flames and out of his mouth a two-edged sword. On His robe and His thigh is written king of kings and lord of lords. He's coming to take His church home. He's coming to deal with the devil once and for all. But before He gets here, He's calling your name. He's saying it's time to remember who you are. It's time to remember Whose you are. It's time to wake up, rise up, and stand in the gap - praying for our families, our friends, and our world.

You're not holding this book by accident. You haven't taken the steps in vain. It's time to reclaim your identity in Christ. It's time to live as Colossians 1:10-14, "So that you may live a life worthy of the Lord and please him in every way; bearing fruit in every good work, growing in the knowledge of God, being strengthened with all power according to his glorious might so that you may have great endurance and patience, and giving thanks to the Father, who has qualified you to share in the inheritance of his holy people in the kingdom of light. For he has rescued us from the dominion of darkness and brought us into the kingdom of the Son he loves, in whom we have redemption, the forgiveness of sins."

Keep stepping, my friends, one step at a time, one day at a time. Remember that He who is in you is greater than he who is in the world. We have victory, and we know how this story ends. Hallelujah!

Annie Bouwman

Acknowlegements

I wish to express my sincerest thanks to my family and friends who continue to encourage me on this ministry journey. To those who have shared their struggles with identity - thank you. I pray this book will solidify our discussions and strengthen your resolve to keep fighting. To Pastor Dale and Jeanne, my mentors, thank you for your continued Godly teachings. To my husband, Kurt, I am grateful for your sacrifice and love and am blessed to travel this road with you. But most importantly, to my God. I am amazed at what You've shown me, the truth You have given me, and the path You have placed me on. I am honored to speak Your truth with love and go wherever You lead. I love you!

Class Notes - Week 1

Class Notes - Week 2

Class Notes - Week 3

Class Notes - Week 4

Class Notes - Week 5

Class Notes - Week 6

Class Notes - Week 7

Made in the USA
Columbia, SC
18 September 2021